With His Stripes We Are Healed!

© Copyright 2011

By; Dr. Earl W. Lacy

Ecclesia Publishing House
Detroit MI 48203
ISBN 13: 978-0997085 617
ISBN 10: 0997085614

Table of Contents

Chapter One

Jehovah-Rapha

"Bless the LORD, O my soul; And all that is within me, bless His holy name! {2} Bless the LORD, O my soul, and forget not all His benefits: {3} Who forgives all your iniquities, Who heals all your diseases, {4} Who redeems your life from destruction, Who crowns you with loving-kindness and tender mercies" ---Psalms 103:1-4 NKJV.

He sent His word and healed them, And delivered them from their destructions--- Psalms 107:20 NKJV.

"He heals the brokenhearted and binds up their wounds"---Psalms 147:3 NKJV.

"Surely He has borne our grief (sicknesses, weakness, and distresses) and carried our sorrows and pains {of punishment}... But He was wounded for our transgressions. He was bruised for our guilt and iniquities; the chastisement {needful to obtain} peace and well-being for us was upon Him, and with the stripes {that wounded} Him, we are healed and made whole" Isaiah 53.4,5 Amplified Bible.

Since the Fall of Adam and Eve in the Garden of Eden, themselves and every human being born into the world has not only an inclination to sin, but a body and mind that is susceptible to old age, sickness, disease and mental illnesses. In this declined state and circumstance of Mankind, the Prophet Isaiah speaks forth the Mind of God to a time when sicknesses, weaknesses and distresses---and of course the sin that brought these calamities upon the bloodline of Adam, would be dealt a final blow.

God is the same in nature as He was in ancient times. It was NEVER His will that we be sick, depressed or miserable. He healed sick people in the Old Testament; He even raised a few from the dead. How much more is He able and willing to heal the sick, since the price for disobedience is paid for; the consequences for Adam's disobedience has been reconciled, "justified by Faith", by a verdict of Not Guilty through the shed blood of His righteous and obedient Son. For through one man's disobedience, many were made sinners, frail and prone to disease, physical and spiritual death; how much more through another Man's faithfulness, can many be made righteous and healed from the out-workings of sin, sickness and disease.

We cannot have peace and well-being when our body is racked with pain, twisted and deformed with disease or wasting away in a Hospice Ward, while waiting for death to claim what's left of our physical body. Neither can our family and friends enjoy their lives while knowing that we are perishing. Doctors do all they can to relieve pain and heal the sick; but at some point they reach the end of their medical knowledge.

But lo and behold! Someone has already paid the price to "obtain our peace and well-being: His Name is Jesus Christ. He is the one that Isaiah boldly announced would not only take our sins away, but the consequences, the outworking of the Original Fall from innocence and Grace, which also brought sicknesses and diseases.

"The Spirit of the Lord is upon Me, Because He has anointed Me {the Anointed One, the Messiah} to preach good news (the Gospel) to the poor; He has sent Me to announce release to the captives and recovery of sight to the blind, to send forth as delivered those who are oppressed {who are downtrodden, bruised, crushed, and broken down by calamity}....And He began to speak to them: Today this scripture has been fulfilled while you are present and hearing" ---Luke 4.18,21 Amp. Bible.

As first recorded in Isaiah 61.1, 2, the Prophet Isaiah saw the vision of the Messiah walking the streets of Jerusalem, as He healed the sick. Now we see Jesus of Nazareth, the embodiment of Jehovah, after receiving from the attendant of the synagogue the Book of Isaiah, stands and reads it aloud. At the end of the passage, Jesus rolled up the book, and sat down.

Everyone fastened their eyes on Him, because of His unusual behavior: Jesus rolled up the book because the writings of the Old Testament methodically led up to this day: The Messiah, the Anointed One was incarnated in the natural realm; and everything that Isaiah prophesied had been fulfilled by Him in the streets of Jerusalem. The entire Old Testament was fulfilled, and the facts of it forever settled and sealed.

Jesus declared that the "Spirit of the Lord", the Holy Spirit was upon Him; and that if anyone needed set free from the yoke of oppression, sickness and bondage, now is the acceptable time. He gave the Word of God----that is the practical and kind intent of the Father's will, plan and purpose for His children----not the traditional, religious version of a God that was legalistic, a God who was unusually angry and anxious to kill them---but a loving, compassionate, caring God who willed that everyone be Saved, healed and delivered from the snares of the wicked One, and his demonic host who brought evil, temptations, sicknesses, diseases and calamity.

It is also interesting to note, that though Jesus was anointed to heal the sick; all power in Heaven and earth was at His command---the presence of doubt and unbelief made Him virtually powerless to heal and display His miraculous powers to a people who had no faith in Him as the Messiah (Luke 4.23-30).

Immediately, to remedy this situation, Jesus began to teach in the synagogues; because the entrance of the Word brings Light and understanding.

For too long, like the Jews in the Bible, we have been taught that God will only heal the obedient and extremely faithful---special people, more often the rich and famous---as the Jews thought that the rich were blessed and the poor were cursed; or, as today, "good" Christians would be healed while others be left to suffer and eventually die from lack of adequate medical care, fate or the curse. But the truth is, God heals the sick, regardless of their relationship with Him. That is, whether they are Saved or not. Yes, God heals Moslems and other non-Christians too. This is because the requirements for getting healed is based upon faith in Jesus Christ's ability to heal the sick; that's all---Period.

"O LORD my God, I cried out to You, And You healed me"---Psalms 30:2 NKJV.

Chapter Two

Faith To Believe

"And Jesus went about all Galilee, teaching in their synagogues, preaching the gospel of the kingdom, and **healing all kinds of sickness and all kinds of disease** among the people"--- Mat. 4.23 NKJV.

"Then Jesus said to the centurion, "Go your way; and **as you have believed**, so let it be done for you." And his servant was healed that same hour"--- Mat. 8:13 NKJV.

"When evening had come, they brought to Him many who were demon-possessed. And He cast out the spirits with a word, and **healed all who were sick**"—Mat. 8:16 NKJV.

There are literally hundreds of scriptures that verify the fact that Jesus Christ healed the sick and drove demons out of people. The Word of God is written for our learning, so that we may be informed of spiritual matters, educated and not perish by our lack of spiritual knowledge.

In our modern world with its Internet super highway, social networks and 24-7 bombardment of massive amounts of information: advertisements, programs, entertainment and Hollywood gossip, it is extremely important that we fill our hearts with faith-inspiring scripture, the right information that will get us, family and friends Saved, healed and set free from demonic spirits and their evil agendas.

This was the problem that Jesus faced in His ministry to the Jews, and He continues to encounters it today, even in the local churches. He finds a people with abundant traditions and knowledge of natural things, but lacking in spiritual faith to believe His entire Word.

Faith to believe in order to get healed is the information most needed. Teaching on the certainty and security of the Word of God is the key to getting permanently healed.

The story of the Roman Centurion is a prime example of the faith required to activate the Healing Anointing that is already sent from Heaven and present on the earth.

The Centurion, being a man in authority and under authority, believed (trusted in and relied on) the principles of his leadership position, the giving and receiving of orders. He said to Jesus, "but speak the word only, and my servant shall be healed" (Mat. 8.1-13). He further stated: "For I am a man under authority, having soldiers under me; and I say to this man, Go! And he goes; and to another, Come, and he comes; and to my servant, Do this, and he does it."

The Bible writer stated that Jesus marveled. Jesus was amazed at the faith level of the Roman, being a Gentile, having no part in the Covenant like the Jews, God's chosen people: "Verily, I say to you, I have not found so great faith, no, not in Israel." Then he settled the matter: "Go your way; and **as you have believed**, so let it be done for you."

The words, "as you have believed" is the underlying principle in receiving your healing. What is believed in the heart is expressed with the mouth and acted upon. If we pray that Jesus would heal us, we are praying that Jesus do something that He has not already done, and it is up to us to accept it by faith, and take authority over the sickness or disease---like the Centurion took authority over the solders and the servant that was given him: They Go when he said to go!

"Why are you fearful, O you of little faith" (Mat. 8.20) This is not the avenue in which to get healed. Jesus recognizes that people have different levels of faith: from "mustard seed" faith too "great faith." So, we should endeavor to have the type of faith that brings the healing power upon us and into us.

"Now when the woman saw that she was not hidden, she came trembling; and falling down before Him, she declared to Him in the presence of all the people the reason she had touched Him and how she was healed immediately"--- Luke 8:47 NKJV.

The woman in this passage, conceived in her heart a plan of direct action to get healed. She believed and was totally sold out on the idea that if she even touched the hem of Jesus' garment, she would receive healing. No amount of obstacles---neither did she discuss the matter with anyone---would impede her; she applied her faith, and made a demand on the supply of healing virtue from Jesus' body, without Him consciously releasing it to her. How much more, since Jesus has consciously released healing into the population, can we readily tap into this Life-Stream. Faith is a Spiritual Law; it will work for everyone!

"Have **faith in God**. For verily I **say** unto you, that whosoever shall **say** unto this mountain, Be removed, and be cast into the sea; and shall **not doubt in his heart**, but shall **believe** that those things which he **says** shall come to pass; he shall have whatsoever he **says.** Therefore, I say unto you, what things you desire, when you pray, **believe** that you receive them, and you shall have them"---Mark 11.22-24.

Certain words have been presented in bold to make a point. Some translations state, "have the faith of God," which is a more accurate translation. God has faith in what He says; He knows that it will come to pass. General faith in God can encompass many erroneous preconceived doctrines and ideas about God, and can even include what other religions believe. But the faith of God is different, because it involves only with God proclaims is true.

From there we examine the word "say" as a command given, an order (like when God said, "Let there be light," or the Centurion said to his soldiers, "Go." Faith, present and active in the heart, produces words upon the lips reflecting what is believed in the heart; this is faith followed by corresponding works---action!

Faith declares that the Word of God is true, and we were, and are healed because of the finished work at Calvary; that God watches over His Word to perform it.

Doubt in the heart produces fear, and Fear is the opposite of faith. Fear declares that the words of the devil, sickness, disease and mental illness are true and permanent; included is the idea that we might as well get used to living in pain and weakness.

"And He said to her, Daughter, be of good cheer; **your faith has made you well.** Go in peace"---Luke 8:48 NKJV.

Jesus didn't say that **His faith** had healed her, but her faith! The measure of faith given her at birth was used.

Let's say that we have money Direct Deposited into our account. When we go to the bank or use our Debit Card, the technical term is that we make a "Demand" on the Deposit (Supply) that is in our account. We are not begging for our money, but simply making a withdrawal.

It's the same with our electrical service: When we plug in and turn on an appliance, we make a Demand upon the Supply of electricity at the power company; so it is with healing: We make a Demand on the Supply of the Holy Spirit that is readily available to us free of charge. That is, free to us, but it cost Jesus at Calvary.

"Now it happened on a certain day, as He was teaching, that there were Pharisees and teachers of the law sitting by, who had come out of every town of Galilee, Judea, and Jerusalem. And **the power of the Lord was present to heal them**"--- Luke 5:17 NKJV.

One would think that wherever Jesus the Person was present, that the power to heal the sick was also. But Luke's observation was accurate in that although Jesus was present, the faith of the audience was not always at the level to activate the Anointing within Him; His hometown, Jerusalem is a prime example of doubt and unbelief quenching the work of the Holy Spirit.

In this particular verse, Luke "perceived" in his spirit that the Holy Spirit was present and working in the audience; and perhaps he saw with his natural eyes and heard with his natural ears, the physical and emotional reactions of the people as they were being healed.

Faith to believe is so important; there is no substitute for faith, inasmuch as it is the only thing that pleases God.

Chapter Three

Salvation and Healing

"Because if you acknowledge and **confess with your lips** that Jesus is Lord and in your **heart believe** (adheres to, trusts in and rely on the truth) that God raised Him from the dead, you will be saved.

For **with the heart, a person believes** (adheres to, trust in and relies on Christ) and so is justified (declared righteous, acceptable to God), and with the mouth he **confesses** (declares openly, and speaks out freely his faith) and **confirms** his salvation" ---Romans 10.9,10 Amp. Bible.

This scripture is primarily quoted for its contents on Salvation---which is its general interpretation. But its specific interpretation is to unveil the authority inherited in our spoken word.

First of all, as stated earlier in this book---when we speak out our mouth what is believed (trusted in and relied on) in the heart, we can bring into reality what we say----be it good or bad. But in this scripture text, we are applying faith of the heart towards spiritual healing.

We confess with our mouth what the Word of God says is the truth---that "with His stripes, we are healed and made whole." And because we believe this with our entire heart (spirit, intellect, emotions and will) it will come to pass. The Holy Spirit (God) is not a respecter of persons.

Healing was purchased at the same time that Salvation was; both are activated and received by faith in the Word of God. And, as stated earlier, a person doesn't even have to accept the Salvation provision to be healed; getting healed is a matter of faith in Jesus Christ the Healer, and not necessary Jesus Christ, the Savior.

And though God truly wants everyone to accept Jesus Christ as their personal Lord and Savior, through His mercy He allows healing to go forth without it. Many times, people are so grateful for being healed that they get Saved too!

The second portion of the scripture states "for with the heart man believes." This has not been taught in the churches as much as it should be: What does it mean to "believe" and what part of us does this take place?

Most of us have head-knowledge---what is called mental accent; we claim that we believe something but fail to act upon it as truth. We more often than not, "think" or rationalize that because we read the Bible, and memorized a few scriptures, or the pastor preached that God heals the sick, that we believe:

But we don't live as though it is absolute truth; and when sick we offer up a simple, half-hearted prayer without genuine faith attached; then we get discouraged and give up---even may go as far as to verbalize that the scriptures concerning healing don't work, or miracles were for the formation of the early church; or we rationalize that, "I'm not eligible to be healed," because of some sin, lifestyle, situation, circumstance, genes, curse or religious reason.

But now we are not like that and refuse to drawl back from receiving all that God has for us. We believe with our entire heart that not only did God raise Jesus from the dead and glorify Him, but that Jesus purchased healing for all of us who will accept and embrace it.

And so, by speaking out what we believe concerning healing, we confirm it. And by the power of our faith-filled words, we call those things that be not as yet, as though they already exist. So, then, faith comes by hearing and the putting into practice the Word of God; and healing comes by believing, embracing it and Christ the Healer, plus the putting into practice the Word of God.

"Now faith is the assurance (the confirmation, the title deed) of the things {we} hope for, being the proof of things {we} do not see and the conviction of their reality {faith perceiving as real fact what is not revealed to the senses} Hebrews 11.1 Amp. Bible.

Above is a technical definition of what Faith is and how it works. Faith, being different from Hope, has for years been taught to be virtually the same thing---when it isn't.

Faith is right NOW, in the present tense. Hope is something in the past or future; and Mental ascent, a mental concept, idea or group of thoughts, exist only in our minds and not in the heart.

Faith of the heart gets us what we Hope for in our minds; meaning, faith is the substance of things hoped for. Our mental-Hope is that we be healed, and our faith obtains (or fetches) the healing for us in the present tense!

Faith is our assurance, our confirmation, our claim-check to what the Word of God states concerning healing our bodies. In the natural, when we purchase something or pay utility bills over the Internet or telephone, we receive a receipt or confirmation number that is proof that we paid the purchasing price or made a payment on it.

Faith, which is also a Spiritual Law, is acceptable proof that we have fulfilled the requirements for healing; it is like the title deed that we receive when we purchase a vehicle or home, which proves that we are the owner.

Faith acts as our conviction of a different and better heavenly reality---an unwavering certainty. Through the eyes of faith, what we hope for is as real (or even more real) as the material world we live in; and this faith of the heart sees beyond the previous days, months or years of sickness and disease---to a completely healed body.

Because all this is hidden from the natural senses until it happens, many of us get discourage. Well don't give up.

"But without faith it is impossible to please Him; for he that comes to God must believe that He is, and that He is a rewarder of them that diligently seek Him" ---Heb. 11.6).

Hebrews Chapter 11, the Hall of Faith, speaks of those who by faith accomplished great things. Several descriptive words are used in the Amplified Bible to illustrate how faith moved people: By faith, prompted by faith, because of faith, actuated by faith, urged on my faith, aroused by faith, and motivated by faith. Faith is the driving force behind their human actions. Faith is still our divine connection to God and His Covenant Promises.

"And one of them, when he saw that he was healed, returned, and with a loud voice glorified God"---Luke 17:15 NKJV. (Story of the ten lepers).

32 "And they were astonished at His doctrine: For His **Word was with power**. 36 And they were all amazed, and spoke among themselves, saying, What a Word is this! For with **authority** and **power** He **commanded** the unclean spirits, and they **come** out. 40 Now when the sun was set-ting, all they that had any sick with different diseases brought them unto Him; and **He laid His hands on every one of them, and healed them**"---Luke 4.32, 36, 40.

Notes

Chapter Four

Authority of the Believer

"Truly, I tell you, whatever you forbid and declare to be improper and unlawful on earth must be what is already forbidden in heaven, and whatever you permit and declare proper and lawful on earth must be what is already permitted in heaven"---Mat. 18.18 Amp. Bible.

Here we discover another description concerning the authority of the Believer in Jesus Christ; but, as I said, Spiritual Laws like the Law of Faith will work for anyone who will make a Demand on the Supply. There isn't any evidence that the woman who touched the hem of Jesus' garment, or the Roman Centurion believed that Jesus was the Christ, the Savior of the world; they basically believed that He could heal them!

The King James Version of the above scripture used the words "bind" and "loose." But the literal and practical application is to "forbid" or "permit."

Since sicknesses, diseases, deformities etc only exist in the natural realm, and not Heaven, we as believers in healing can declare them as improper and unlawful to operate in our daily lives.

There is no sin-principle or demons to administer decline, calamity or temptation in Heaven; the sin-principle and demonic presence and activities are forbidden, forever locked out of Heaven with the one who created them---Satan.

Now, the latter portion of the scripture states what we permit or declare to be lawful in our lives---health for instance—has to be according to what is established and permitted in Heaven. We come into agreement with the laws of Heaven---what proceeds out of the mouth of God, what the Word of God states and its dominate Spiritual Laws that Govern what God says.

Another point to make is that the action must first take place on earth, before Heaven will respond and back us up. If we are satisfied with being sick, then Heaven and its Spiritual Laws will not interfere, neither will the Holy Spirit who is amongst us on Earth heal us if we don't want it.

And since the devil doesn't hold any office in Heaven, he doesn't have any authority there, we as Believers in Christ the Healer, who are also seated in the heavens at the throne of God, and in Christ--- can demand from that lofty position that sickness be gone out of our bodies: Say, 'Loose me---in the Name of Jesus Christ!'

"And when He had called His twelve disciples to Him, He gave them **power over unclean spirits**, to cast them out, and to **heal all kinds of sickness and all kinds of disease**"---Matthew 10:1 NKJV.

"Heal the sick, cleanse the lepers, raise the dead, cast out demons. Freely you have received, freely give--- Matthew 10:8 NKJV.

Religious folk will say, "but Jesus gave this authority to the Twelve Apostles----He gave these miracles to start the church. But why would Jesus do that? Show miracles, signs and wonders to lure people into His family, and then stop, abandoning His disciples to suffer sickness and disease under the tyranny of the devil? Jesus doesn't use "bait and switch" schemes! He is the same yesterday, today, and forever.

We're entitled to our personal opinions, but not our personal truth, concerning the healing of the sick.

There were religious folk in Jesus' ministry. They were called Pharisees and Sadducees. In Luke 7.4-7, the Jews came to Jesus to ask for the healing of the Roman Centurion's servant. They said, "That he was **worthy** for He should do this: For he loves our nation, and has built us a synagogue." Truly a noble deed for a Gentile.

 But he Centurion knew how authority works. He stated, "Wherefore, neither thought I myself worthy to come unto thee; but **say in a word**, and my servant shall be healed."

See the difference? The religious Jews depended on good deeds, being worthy, to receive favor and healing from God; but the Centurion knew that getting his servant healed was a matter of faith, the power and command of spiritually-charged words.

"Again I say unto you, that if two of you shall **agree on earth** as touching anything that they shall ask, it shall be done for them of My Father which is in heaven" Mat. 18.19.

Jesus often used the word "again" because He had taught this principle in other discourses using other examples. We can be healed through our individual faith in the Word of God; we can also be healed through the Prayer of Agreement, or two or more persons of faith believing in the healing power of the Savior.

First, this agreement takes place on earth, before God in Heaven and the Spiritual Law of Faith activates. This principle also works on situations and circumstances other than healing---but since this book is primarily about healing, we will stick close to that.

Through the Prayer of Agreement, the overall authority of the individual Believer is multiplied---even amplified---when two or more agree on the Word of God; specifically what is accepted in heaven as the eternal will of God, being by Faith accepted and decreed on earth.

So, our faith-filled words as a Believer can send a thousand demons of sickness and disease running for parts unknown; and two or more Believers can scatter ten thou-sand demons.

Seeking healing according to the Word of God is how healing is obtained. Deviating from the Word of God can bring into effect doubt, unbelief, religion, witchcraft, heresy, old wives' tales and people's religious opinions.

Many churches fall short in what is required of them. They spend the majority of ministry time talking about money; but quickly collect names and put them on a Prayer List. Being prayed for in person generates faith.

Oftentimes, no one even takes the time to pray for those named on the lists; or the person who is assigned to pray views it as merely a formality, or another task to perform before the shift ends. Many in these prayer positions (not true Prayer Intercessors) lack the understanding, conviction and faith to believe that Jesus heals the sick. Nevertheless, many depend on this type of proxy when we can also pray for ourselves and believe!

And although a Phone Prayer Line is better than nothing, it is closer to scripture that we seek Christian professionals; and also seek medical professionals to render their education and experience, for God is pleased to work through medical professionals--- even surgeons--- and prescription medicines to bring about complete healings of His children. God will give the medical treatment an extra "zing" to make it work faster and better. Remember, Luke the beloved Physician, traveled and worked with the Apostle Paul, who was a spiritual healer.

"Is anyone among you sick? Let him call for the elders of the church, and let them pray over him, anointing him with oil in the name of the Lord. {15} And the prayer of faith will save the sick, and the Lord will raise him up. And if he has committed sins, he will be forgiven. {16} Confess your trespasses to one another, and pray for one another, that you may be healed. The effective, fervent prayer of a righteous man avails much" --- James 5:14-16 NKJV.

The above scripture was written to the churches. Although healing is available to everyone, the instruction and obligation of those who want to be healed is to contact the elders of the church---those who are well-informed concerning the healing provisions.

The sick are to be prayed for, anointed with blessed oil in the Name (Reputation) of Jesus Christ. The prayer that is motivated, actuated, prompted and propelled by faith will heal the sick.

Now the next verses should be considered in light of the entire Word of God concerning how sickness and disease originated on earth and in the human situation: The prayer concerning sin and forgiveness is to release us from any claims that the devil has against us, legal rights--- generational curses passed on through the bloodline and mutated genes---that he might have to inflict us with calamity and woe; plus it releases us from any unforgiveness that we may hold against others.

By confessing known sins, God is then able to release and forgive us from any un-repented sins, whereby paving the way for the Holy Spirit to replace the darkness with Light, clearing the human conscious and promoting health.

Verse 16 in the Amplified Bible states it this way: "The earnest (heartfelt, continued) prayers of a righteous man makes tremendous power available {dynamic in its working}. Tremendous power is what's needed to rid our body from cancer, heart troubles, AIDS and other diseases. Great faith is preferred but many with little faith have gotten out of the deathbed.

"So when Peter saw it, he responded to the people: "Men of Israel, why do you marvel at this? Or why look so intently at us, as though by our own power or godliness we had made this man walk?" --- Acts 3:12 NKJV.

After Jesus gave Believers in Him power over unclean spirits, to cast them out and to heal all sicknesses and diseases, the Apostles went forth to demonstrate this divine unction. When they did, the people, many believing in false gods and idols tried to worship them---something that even the holy angels refuse to accept.

Immediately, the apostles taught the people that it was "Christ in them" who is the Healer. This began the age of Spiritual Gifts, endowments of power, being distributed, severally, by the wisdom of the Holy Spirit as He wills.

"And they that were vexed with unclean spirits; and they were healed. And the whole multitude sought to touch Him; for there went **virtue** out of Him, and **healed them all**" ---Luke 6.18,19.

Not healed some of them, but healed all of them. Virtue went out of Jesus' body because people of faith made a Demand on the Supply, the storehouse flowing from God. There is no end to the creative healing miracles that can manifest when faith is present; even to the lengthening and growth of new limbs and inner organs!

"There came also a multitudes out of the cities round about unto Jerusalem, bringing sick folks, and them which were vexed with unclean spirits; and they were **healed every one**" ---Acts 5.16 (The Apostles heal the sick).

"And now I say unto you, Refrain from these men, and let them alone: For if this teaching or this work be of men, it will come to nothing: But if it be of God, you cannot overthrow it; lest you are fighting against God"---Acts 5.38, 39 (Gamaliel warns the Sanhedrin Council).

Notes

Chapter Five

Gifts of Healing

"To another Faith by the same Spirit, to another Gifts of Healings by the same Spirit" 1 Corinthians 12:9 NKJV.

Definition: The Gifts of Healing are a manifestation of the Holy Spirit in the sphere of disease. It's not "mind over matter" but supernatural. Gifts of Healing are those healings which God effects by His Holy Spirit. They are NOT to be confused with any human abilities (though God may guide a doctor or surgeon's hand and assist them, it is not this gift operating), but a gift given to the Church for the purpose of removing sicknesses, diseases and infirmities that are the results of Adam's Fall or demonic activity.

The term "gifts" is plural. It signifies that the manifestation of the Spirit has several operations: It is a **gift of gifts**, like a cluster of grapes hanging on the vine. As there are classes of diseases: Nerves, muscular, skin, organ, bone, blood, mental etc, so each of the Gifts of Healing has a counteracting effect on some class or ailment.

Examples: Elisha manifested this gift and healed Naaman the Syrian of leprosy; Isaiah healed Hezekiah; Moses through the proxy of the bronze serpent healed the snake-bitten Israelites; Jesus and His disciples healed literally thousands (Jn. 3.14).

The Gifts of Healing are often manifested through the **Laying on of Hands** (Mk. 6.5); by the spoken Word (Mt. 8.8); the sacred healing power can be retained and distributed through common fabric (Acts 19.11,12); the Apostle Peter's shadow was used to manifest the Healing Anointing (Acts 5.15).

Sometimes virtue flows unconsciously from the human reservoir, as for instance when the woman touched the hem of Jesus' garment.

There are a variety of sicknesses and diseases from which the human race suffers. These possibly can be divided into **twelve groups**, which could also mean there are **twelve Gifts of Healing**. The Book of revelation refers to the **Tree of Life bearing twelve manner of fruit whose leaves are for the healing of the nations** (Rev. 22.1,2).

Naaman the Leper

A very interesting story is recorded in Chapter Five of 2 Kings. There was a captain named Naaman over the entire Syrian Army. He was a mighty man of valor, but he also had the disease known as Leprosy.

Anyone who had Leprosy was believed to be cursed, because there was no known medical cure. In Israel, those with Leprosy were forced to leave their homes and city to live in isolation or in a leper colony. Fortunate for Naaman, a Gentile, he lived in Syria.

A servant girl from Israel told Naaman's wife that there was a prophet in Samaria that could heal Naaman. Word got to the king of Syria, and he send a letter to the king of Israel, and Naaman saddled up for the trip to Samaria.

Arriving at Samaria with his horses and chariots at Elisha the Prophets house, Naaman expected Elisha to come out and personally display the awesome power of God and heal him. But instead, Elisha sent Gehazi, his servant out to meet Naaman.

"Go and wash in the Jordan seven times, and your flesh shall come again to you, and you shall be clean" (v. 10)

Naaman was angry and went away. "Behold, I thought he would surly come out to me, and stand, and call upon the Name of the LORD his God, and strike the hand over the place, and remove the leprosy. Are not Abana and Pharpar, rivers of Damascus, better than all the waters of Israel? May I not wash in them, and be clean?" (v. 11).

Naaman's servant didn't come all this way to see his master make such a senseless error. He know that God often works in what seems to be the foolishness of man's limited wisdom.

"And his servant came near, and spoke unto him, and said: My father, if the prophet had bid you to do some great thing, would you not have done it? How much rather then, when he says to you, Wash and be clean?"

Naaman swallowed his pride, went down to the muddy Jordan River, dipped himself seven times, "and his flesh came again like unto the flesh of a little child, and he was clean" (v. 14).

First of all, Naaman was not a Jew and had no provision in the Old Testament Covenant. He had faith to travel to Samaria for his healing. He fell short---as many Christians do---in believing that we are "special" in the sense of our titles, positions, careers or wealth; our medical diagnosis and history is much more complex and difficult than most.

Elisha is a type of Christ. Many of us fail to receive healing from the "servants" of God, but want God (or Jesus) Himself to come down from the throne and heal us. When Jesus doesn't manifest in His Glorified Body, we are not cooperative enough to be healed, and are internally angry at God like Naaman was "wroth" at Elisha for not giving him preferential treatment: Ordinary water will not remove leprosy, cancer or deformities; but God uses natural things---even foolish things---to confound the demonic kingdom with its sicknesses, diseases, oppression and calamity.

Sometimes we make getting ourselves healed harder than it really is. Like Naaman, we expect to perform some great task, when all we really need to do is obey the scriptures as given by the healing school instructor (Elisha).

Naaman wanted a cleaner stream to bath in, when the two cleaner streams he named would have made his body feel fresh and clean, but the end results would be he failed to follow God's instructions to get healed, and the leprosy would remain untouched.

It is a scriptural fact, that Jesus Christ gave His authority to the Believer in Him; He doesn't have to---and seldom does---come down and personally heal us; but in the Spirit, He's present as the Holy Spirit within the one who is ministering, and His Anointing will breech from the human vessel when the Demand is made on it, to destroy yokes, effect healings and obtain lasting cures.

There is a lot more packed into this story including the greedy scheme of Gehazi who pimped the anointing that flowed in the ministry of Elisha; Gehazi went behind Elisha's back and received money and garments that Elisha refused to take from Naaman as payment for the healing. For this, the leprosy of Naaman cleaved to Gehazi and his bloodline. Healing is a work of Grace--- unmerited favor.

Why Do We get Sick?

Since we are exploring the scriptures on the subject of sicknesses and diseases, it is fitting to take a look at why we get sick in the first place.

As stated earlier, when Adam disobeyed God, he lost his innocence. That is, he lost his god-like immortality and because a mortal being. Being mortal subjected him to heat, cold, accidents, injuries---stomach and indigestion issues, and old age.

To make a long list of possibilities short---he and his descendants (us) could contract any of the diseases that we see today; and though some diseases, like Small Pox has been eradicated from the entire earth, many debilitating diseases and viruses remain active and infectious.

So, the majority of the human population today are sick because of generational bloodline genetics (also called Generational Curses). This list includes (but not limited to) such culprits as heart disease, high blood pressure, sugar diabetics, blindness, deafness, muscular dystrophy, sickle cell anemia and other blood disorders, mental illnesses, and most cancers.

Next we discover that many are sick because of environment and workplace hazards, including (but not limited to) asbestos in factories, workplace, office and home. Chemicals in the workplace; old lead paint we ingested as children, chemical spills in the soil on playgrounds, parks and streams; automobile and factory air pollution, and rare jungle-oriented viruses like Ebola.

This list also includes former and present prescription drugs that we took (or still take) for an ailment; many of these drugs had (and still have) serious consequences, side effects that may have been passed on to our unborn children through blood and chromosomal deformities. Many of the pharmaceutical companies knew of these side effects but said nothing in order to slide by the Food and Drug Administration as to make a huge profit. Now they are required to list the side effects even in their commercials. Often the side effects are worst than the medical problem.

Last but not least, we have the "self-inflicted" reasons why we are sick; this includes (but again not limited to) not eating the right foods---poor nutrition, lack of exercise, alcohol and drug abuse, sexual immorality (venereal diseases, HIV, AIDS, Hepatitis A,B,C) worry, anxiety, fear, criminal activity, getting stabbed or shot, taking unnecessary risks, accidents, carelessness, and other ways to shorten our lives or seriously injure our bodies!

Here, I might add: If we go to the hospital with a broken arm, the doctor many inquire how we broke it, but he will not refuse treatment on the grounds that we were careless and broke our arm. Doctors are professional who take an oath to heal people. Even so, The Great Physician, doesn't refuse to heal us because we may have caused the problem ourselves. True, sometimes we are sick because of our sinful lifestyles, but Jesus' healings are not based upon our sin, the sin-principle, or justice---but His Love, Grace and Mercy.

Five Reasons Why Jesus Heals Us.

Considering what has been stated above, it's a miracle that we are still alive. There are so many ways to die, and our bodies can't take but so much pain or disease before it ceases to function. It's good to know that healing is available to all, no matter how we contracted the disease or illness; whether by curse, environment or self-inflicted, Jesus heals them all!

1.   **Jesus imitates the Father:** Jesus Christ is the spiritual incarnation of the Old Testament Jehovah, LORD. When Jesus walked the dusty trails of Israel and the surrounding countryside, on several occasions He told the people that as His Father works, He works. Jesus healed the sick because He imitated the Father's Old Testament healing ministry and whatever the Father did, Jesus did. That is why it is said, "Jesus Christ, the same yesterday, today and forever" ---Hebrews 13.8.

Today, Jesus heals the sick according to the New Testament Covenant, sealed in His own shed blood----even before the Calvary Cross----He received the stripes that healed us. Now we have the right and privilege to boldly approach the throne of Grace to obtain Mercy and find Grace to help in the time of our need.

2. **To Confirm the Covenant:** God watches over the words and promises of His Covenant to perform it; and He's zealous to perform His Word. Jesus heals the sick because God promised it in His Word. "I am the Lord who heals you," He states. God's Covenants He will not break or alter the thing once it is given. "Blessed be the LORD, that has given rest to His people Israel, according to all that He promised; there has not failed one word of all His good promises"--- 1 Kings 8.56. Both Old and New Testament Covenants contain healing promises that were consummated and fulfilled when He died on the cross.

3. **His Agape Love:** Agape Love is the highest form of love; it is pure love; it is God, for God is Love. This same love for mankind is

displayed in the willingness of Jesus Christ the Healer to heal the sick; His great compassion moves Him to heal all that are oppressed by the devil. It is the same compassion and tender-heartedness that moves Him to save the lost from eternal dam-nation, motivates Him to heal the sick and afflicted.

He is not willing that any should perish through sickness or disease, or to be spiritually and eternally lost. "For God so loved (Agape) the world, that He gave His only begotten Son, so that whosoever believes in Him should not perish, but shall have everlasting Life" ---John 3;16.

4. **His righteousness:** Jesus heals the sick because it's a righteous thing to do; it's good faith followed by good works. How can a loving and caring God who makes covenants with us, not do anything about our torments and the human misery of sickness and disease, and still maintain His integrity, His righteousness, His Wonderful Name?

Nevertheless, it's not His personality and nature to make us obey His Word, follow instructions, or have faith to believe in healing or anything else He has provided for us. In short, we can remain sick, if that is what we want; or we can be healed, because that is what we (and He) want. Shall not the Judge of all the earth do right?" Gen. 18.25. Yes, He will do what is right!

5. **To Destroy the works of the Devil:** Since the Fall in the Garden of Eden, sickness, disease and calamity has run rampant throughout the generations of mankind. Though there were notable healings and miracles in the Old Testament, the time had not yet come for the Messiah to address the Adamic Sin issue, and the progressive outflow of daily personal sins of the generations of Adam.

Since sickness and disease came into the human race through one man's sin (Adam), it was dealt with and taken away by another Man's (Jesus') obedience to the Father. In the wisdom of God, the course of sicknesses and disease was allowed to run its spiritual course until it was at its peak---then God cut it off forever at the cross of His dear Son. So, in reality, sicknesses and diseases are spiritually done away with; we just have to appropriate the knowledge and activate our faith by practicing it: Call those things that be now as yet as though they already exist! Then we will receive healing. "For this purpose the Son of God was manifested, that He might destroy the works of the devil"---1 John 3.8.

This is the age of miracles, signs and wonders. We are in position to receive all that God has promised---even before the foundation of the world. Miracles of healings are but a breath away; breathe in the Holy Spirit, and exhale whatever sickness, disease or infirmity that is keeping you from obtaining the next level in your destiny.

It is the Father's good pleasure to heal you; for it pleased Him to separate us from the world and make us a member of His family. God loves us, and He knows that our pain is keeping us from focusing on Him and experiencing joy unspeakable and full of glory. God has made healing us personal.

"And when he (blind Bartimacus) heard that it was Jesus of Nazareth, he began to cry out, and say, Jesus, Son of David, have mercy on me. And many told him that he should **he should keep quiet,** but he cried the more a great deal, Son of David, have mercy on me. Jesus stood still and commanded him to be called...And he, casting away his garment, rose, and came to Jesus. And Jesus answered and said unto him, What do you want Me to do for you? The blind man said unto Him, Lord, that I might receive my sight. And Jesus said unto him, Go your way, **your faith has made you whole**"---Mark 10.47-52.

We have to be like Bartimacus when it comes to getting healed. People told him to shut up and be content that he wasn't dead!

But Blind Bart was determined to be healed; he didn't care what the crowd had to say; they weren't blind, begging and stumbling around Jerusalem. Bart had faith to believe that when Jesus called him, he would have no further need for the blind person's cloak; he casted it off, and soon after his blindness was cast off and returned to the pit of hell where it came from.

"For I tell you, that many prophets and kings have desired to see those things which you see, and have not seen them, and to hear those things that you hear, and have not heard them" Luke 10.24 .

Notes

Chapter Six

Demonic Interference

As stated earlier sicknesses and diseases can be transferred many ways---germs, bacteria and virus can be transferred via a sneeze by a passing stranger, or touching contaminated objects. In this chapter, we will discuss how sicknesses, diseases, genetics and general curses play an unseen role in making us sick and keeping us in that state.

Face it, being sick is not God's will at all; it is demonic activity. Remember, not all sickness is the results of an indwelling demon spirit, but it's always a possibility. This is because a spirit of infirmity causes a physical or mental manifestation in the body. Here are a few scriptural accounts where the problem is identified as an indwelling spirit (s):

1. Boy with dumb and deaf spirit. Mark 9.14-26.

2. Demons are driven out of sick people. Luke 4.40,41.

3. Insane man has legion of demons. Luke 8.26-35.

Although there are hundreds of symptoms of demonic interference, some of which have their root in emotional and medical disorders that may be chemical or electrical related, a physician should always be consulted. As these lists are only a guideline to recognizing problems, it is not meant to be conclusive or a substitute for medical attention.

Failure to get healed after fasting and prayer, unexplained illness with no diagnosis, including rashes. Chronic depression, suicide attempts, hostile behavior, seizures, suddenly compelled to go places, cutting the flesh, excessive compulsive behaviors, eating disorders, mental illnesses (all types), hearing voices, superhuman strength, terror in the mind, recurring nightmares, flashbacks, seeing evil spirits,

Jesus is the Great Physician. He said, "Ask and you shall receive. It is always to our best interest to do what Jesus says. But often times, we find it all but impossible to obey His Word. These are times when the influences of the demonic kingdom, family, friends and religious folks are at their worst in our lives.

It is beneficial to our spiritual growth to find a trusted, dedicated, non-judgmental professional to get help; a ministry empowered by the Holy Spirit and devoted to setting the captives free, is what's needed; not a gossiper or busybody. We should pray and ask God to direct us to someone whom He uses to release and activate Physical Healing, Emotional Healing, Deliverance and Restoration.

Other areas in our lifestyle may get in the way of our faith and complete healing. As demons can be the motivating intelligence behind things we do and decisions we make, they can also block attempts made to heal the body. This is NOT always the case; but repentance of sins and forgiving those we have grudges against will release us to be more open and susceptible to the healing power.

Secret sins, past traumas and negative childhood experiences are not volcanoes but the effect are often the same. Those urges that we suppress, fail to suppress and indulge in behind closed doors may take its toll on the mind and body. Below are a few "volcanoes" and manifestations of demonic activity. Fear, worry, sickness and disease, chronic pain, Crack/cocaine/heroin, pre-scription drug addiction, Marijuana, cigarettes, psychological addictions, gambling, rejection, rebellion, guilt, shame, pride stress, bitterness, jealousy, violence, road rage, criminality, stealing, overeating, laziness, procrastination, cursing, suicide, self hatred, lust abandonment, depression, obsession, emotional abuse, physical abuse, sexual abuse, incest, abortion, fornication, adultery, pornography, homosexuality, Lesbianism, Pedophilia, masturbation, fetishes, necrophilia, bestiality, forgetfulness, curses, hearing voices mental illness, paranoia, hatred of men, hatred of women, spousal abuse, witchcraft, demonic interference, cults, religious error, problems concentrating, can't solve simple problems.

It is amazing what can go on mentally or physically within us and our lifestyles! Anything in the above list could be grounds for demons to have a legal right due to our willful participation in sin. Then when the Healing Power of God comes in contact with our body, resistance from within tries to keep things the way they are.

Fortunately, God is more powerful than any spirit or group of spirits. Inner Healing and Deliverance cleans out the demons, so that the healing power can repair the damaged left behind.

Demons are like a Rock Band tearing up a hotel room, and leaving the hotel management to clean the place up after they leave. The Holy Spirit is who cleans us up.

Many of us fail to realize that demons have been on the earth thousands of years before we were born. This means that they have had plenty of time to master their trade before we showed up! Inner healing and Deliverance is the children's bread; where basic physical healing is recommended and practical for those who haven't accepted Jesus Christ as their personal Lord and Savior.

Inner Healing takes place when we pour out our heart to God; we empty ourselves of our own plans, hopes, ambitions, pride and self-sufficiency and ask God to search our entire heart, the deepest recesses and territory within us, to bind up our broken hearts and comfort our morning, and provide the oil of gladness, a garment of praise instead of the spirit of discouragement and despair; to drive out the enemy and set fire to his camp---the fire of the Holy Ghost---and set us at liberty, who have been bruised, abused and bound hand and foot by dark chains.

The healing of past hurts and torn emotions will effect a lasting change in the way we think and feel. The renewing of the mind and the balancing of the intellect, emotions, will and imagination will revitalize the physical body too; the removal of unclean spirits, strongholds, delusions, vain imaginations, and thinking distortions will make us the New Creature mentioned in the scriptures. Before we know it, the mind will quiet and have less background chatter going on (demons are gone, no more secret board meetings). And we will be able to sleep soundly, awaken refreshed, and have an intimate relationship with God. New life radiating inside brings healing to the outside.

God said that His people perish because of a lack of knowledge. There is an old saying that "what we don't know won't hurt us." I'm here to state that millions of us perish each year because we are unaware of the invisible spiritual forces that operate against our mortal lives; and in the natural, that's all we have is one life to live.

There are also millions of harmful viruses, bacteria and germs that can attack the physical body, especially when our immune system is compromised, and vulnerable by a severe illness. People have been known to contract life-threatening infections from the hospital room or equipment! My point isn't to scare anyone, but to point out the need to trust in the Lord with all our hearts and not lean on our own understanding, or depend entirely on science to solve our health problems.

We need to know the value and certainty of the Word of God to protect us from the visible, invisible and the microscopic. One of the most powerful weapons in our warfare is prayer.

Prayer changes things; it doesn't change God because He "changes not." So, therefore, it's no longer up to Him who gets healed because healing has been released into the earth! But prayer can change the situations and circumstances in our lives. Prayer can bring into manifestation on Earth the perfect will of God---"Thy will be done on Earth as it is in Heaven." That is how the Lord Jesus put it; that's God's perfect will---living in divine health---be manifested on the Earth too.

Scripturally, we do not ask God to heal us, because according to His Word, He healed us at the cross over 2000 years ago. What we do is appropriate, simply accept by faith what was already done as a **FINISHED WORK**.

But if we should pray and ask God to heal us, minimum faith is released because we believe that **He will heal us**, **instead of He has healed us**. The latter releases more faith; the former is a mixture of hope-faith, instead of pure faith. Believing that God will heal us is far better than believing that He won't heal us; But perfect faith is believing God through Jesus Christ has already healed us.

So praying that God will heal us is a prayer He will accept when we are babes in Christ; but at some point, He expects us to spiritually mature in our understanding and practice of the Word of God. The release of maximum faith makes a strong Demand on the Healing Anointing.

Types of Prayers

There are many types of prayers and ways to pray; since this is not a book on prayer, we will only discuss a few types as it pertains to Healing, Inner Healing and Deliverance; the last extreme is often necessary.

The Prayer of Faith is described in many ways and places in the New Testament. Prayer for the Christian is based on the New Testament Covenant. It is under Grace, forgiveness and mercy. It is through the New Testament Covenant, an agreement brokered by Jesus Christ and Jehovah-Elohim, the Father, that our healing comes.

In Mk. 11.24 it states, "Therefore I tell you, whatever you ask for in prayer, believe that you have received it, and it will be yours." Believe that we are healed and it will manifest in our body. Jesus proclaimed, "Have Faith in God." Another translation says, "Have the Faith of God," which also makes sense because God does everything through the exercise of His Faith. He has dealt to everyone a measure, a degree, a mustard seed of His divine Faith.

God, through Faith, calls those things that be not as though they already were; this is the Healing Prayer based and rooted in Faith---to call those things that be not as yet as though they already exist and are manifested.

In Eph. 6.10-17, the Apostle Paul gave a discourse on spiritual warfare. From there he immediately wrote of prayer being an essential part of that spiritual warfare: "Pray at all times (on every occasion, in every season) in the Spirit, with all {manner of} prayer and entreaty" Eph 6.18 (Amp).

The Prayer of Consecration is another type of prayer that is widely described and used in the New Testament Covenant. To consecrate means to sanctify, separate for a divine purpose. We as Christians are a people set aside by God. We are members of His divine family, the Church, the Bride of Christ, the fruit, being the children of the Resurrection.

Therefore, we are separated from the world, and do separate ourselves by uttering this type of prayer. We declare and decree aloud that we belong to Christ and He belongs to us! If there is some unholy practice in our lives, repent, be released from it, and it won't have the power to interfere with our healing.

In the upper room, Jesus consecrated the wine and the bread through prayer. "And as they were eating, Jesus took bread, and blessed it, and brake it, and gave it to the disciples, and said, "Take, eat, this is my body. And He took the cup, and gave thanks, and gave it to them, saying, Drink ye all of it. For this is my blood of the New Testament" (Mat. 28.26-28). In Jn. 17.15-17 (Amp. Bible),

Jesus consecrated, set apart disciples for a special purpose: "I do not ask that You take them out of the world, but that You will keep and protect them from the evil one. They are not of the world (worldly, belonging to the world), {just} as I am not of the world. Sanctify them {purify, consecrate, separate them for Yourself, make them holy} by the Truth; Your word is Truth."

In further verses, Jesus consecrated Himself and future Believers in the Body of Christ, so that we are also sanctified, purified, separated and wholly consecrated to and In Him. In the same way the Father sent Jesus into the world, Jesus sends us into the world with the same Anointing to heal and be consecration through prayer.

It makes no difference if we are ministers or being ministered to, separation from sinful practices, mental pollution or just time-wasting practices will help the minister to heal more people---and faster---and help us who need healing to be more receptive.

Deliverance Prayer

Heavenly Father, I humble myself before You in the Name of Jesus Christ. I confess my sins; I am sorry for every one of them. I have accepted Jesus Christ as my Lord and Savior. I am redeemed by the Blood of Jesus and accept Forgiveness Inner Healing and Deliverance. Lord, through the power of the Holy Spirit, completely cleanse me. I have unwisely allowed (Name the unclean spirit(s) to gain access, oppress, torment and use me.

I seek to recover my freedom, wholeness, and to exercise free will over my spirit, soul, mental facilities, will, intellect, emotions, imagination and physical body, to be set free of all infirmities and influences of unclean spirits. I denounce Satan and his plans, purposes, and pursuits. I separate myself from Satan and claim refuge in the Lord Jesus Christ. I demand and decree my immediate release from all evil spirits and influences operating in my life.

In Jesus' Name, I exercise my will and Christian Authority over evil spirits assigned to harass, steal, kill and destroy me. I bind and break your power, strongholds, thinking distortions, delusions, addictions and influences in the Name of Jesus.

BY NOW FAITH: In the Name of Jesus Christ, I NOW declare that you unclean spirits are unlawfully encroaching according to the Word of God: I demand that you leave me! I am a child of God. I declare: Depart from me you cursed spirits!

BY NOW FAITH: I claim the promises: (Joel 2.32) "That whosoever shall call upon the Name of the Lord shall be delivered." The Word cleanses me from all sin. I am a holy temple of God; and Greater is He within me than he that is in the world. I belong to Christ and Him only will I serve. Lord Jesus Christ, right NOW, I accept my Healing and Deliverance. Fill me, Lord, with your Holy Spirit. Bless the Name of Jesus. Amen!

Prayer Of Dominion

Father, in the Name of Jesus, I take spiritual authority against the Principalities, Powers, Rulers of the Darkness and Spiritual Wickedness in the heavenly places assigned to this region. I exercise dominion against all demonic manipulations, control, influences and strongholds. I declare them to be unlawfully assembled according to the Word of God.

Therefore in the Name and by the Blood of Jesus, I render their works bound in the earth as they are in Heaven. In Jesus' Name, I openly declare that every manifestation, operation, assignment or maneuver of the enemy against me or my bloodline has become ineffective and made void. I exercise dominion against all evil spirits assigned to steal, kill and destroy my body or soul.

In the Name and by the Blood of Jesus Christ, I bind all unclean spirits, including sicknesses, diseases, depression, tormenting, perversion, lying, racism, hatred, unforgiveness, rebellion, religion, legalism, condemnation, guilt, unbelief, shame, rejection, abandonment, abuse, inferiority, rejection, greed, drug and alcohol addictions, violence, pornography, sexual perversions, sin ---plus every spirit that binds and oppresses me.

BY NOW FAITH, I activate the Blood of Jesus over me I declare the Blood to be a witness against the territorial spirit activity and their eternal defeat. I now release Healing and Deliverance in the Name of Jesus from all bondages and declare and decree myself free to serve the Lord Jesus Christ with wholeness and soundness of mind.

BY NOW FAITH, I declare that I am blessed and open to the Spirit of God, sensitive to the voice of the Holy Spirit, the Word and the will of God. I decree that where sin abounds that Grace much more abounds, that the Life and Light of Christ prevails against the darkness of Satan, that truth prevails against decepception; Healing and Deliverance prevails against bondage, and obedience prevails against rebellion.

Father, I thank and praise You that Your Kingdom has come and Your will is being done in the earth as it is in Heaven. I declare in the Name of Jesus that my body is the temple of the Holy Spirit and He dwells within; I am separated for Your purpose.

Holy Spirit, fall upon me and come out of my spirit and make Your Presence known. To Jesus be honor and glory forever, amen.

Praying In Tongues

"For he that speaks in an unknown tongue, speaks not unto men, but unto God; for no man understands him, howbeit in the Spirit he speaks mysteries. 1 "But you, beloved, building up yourself on your most holy faith, praying in the Holy Ghost" ---1 Cor. 14.4; Jude 1.20. Praying in Tongues is the last type of prayer to be discussed in this chapter. This phenomenon is strictly a New Testament manifestation of the Holy Spirit. Over the years there has been much controversy concerning the Baptism in/with the Holy Spirit, accompanied by the scriptural evidence of speaking in other/ unknown tongues (Acts.2.4).

Nevertheless, praying in Tongues is the manifestation of the Holy Spirit within, and this is the Spirit of Jesus; He is also Christ the Healer.

If you believe what you have read: Whatever limitation---wheelchair or walker---leave it like Blind Bart did---and walk away from it!

Whatever, sickness or disease you have---ignore it---And Be healed in Jesus Name!

The End

(Of your sickness and disease.)

www.ingramcontent.com/pod-product-compliance
Lightning Source LLC
Chambersburg PA
CBHW071752020426
42331CB00008B/2287